Be a Self-taught woodworker

Turn the basics into anything you can think of.

by Chris Hattan

Thanks for
the chat

C Hattan

Get your free video instructions here

3 FREE
Videos

As part of this book, I've created a 3 video course to learn the basic woodworking joints

Then turn these joints into anything you can think of!

https://www.kingbespokecreations.uk/be-a-self-taught-woodworker

To Liesle and Eloise

Prologue

I'm a normal guy. I have a family, a home and food on the table. I'm not a self-made millionaire or award winning entrepreneur. I passed my exams at school and have never been to jail. Statistically, I'm extremely average!

So what authority do I have to write a book on self learning and woodwork? Well the simple answer is that I have been a self-taught woodworker for over 20yrs. Add to that I truly believe in being self-taught, that structured education isn't for everyone and regularly doesn't help us to understand a subject, rather it gets us to learn specific parts to pass a test.

Living in the western world, I'm very fortunate to have a full school education. Don't ever think I want to change that. However I never used to see the point of it all while I was there. Apparently when I was around 5 years of age I returned home from school and declared to my Mum

"I can read and write now Mummy, so I don't need to go back to school"!

Very rarely could anyone tell me the practical uses for the information I was learning. Even when I went to university to study Physiology. I asked my tutor if he could give me some examples of the kinds of jobs I could get with this degree. The answer came with a questioning shrug,

"Erm... research work?"

He couldn't tell me! Why would I sit there for 3 years with no target to aim for and no purpose for the information I was trying to understand? I lasted 6 months before dropping out and heading home.

My first career was as a landscape gardener. This happened almost by chance when I quit university and helped out a chap who needed an extra pair of hands for a big job. By the end of the first day he offered me a full time position.

Andy was a brilliant 'boss'. I use that term lightly as he rarely told me what to do. There were tasks that needed doing and I would often get the chance to think for myself and figure out how to arrange the order of things. After a few years my brother joined us and when Andy was offered a job to manage a garden centre (plants were always his first love) my brother and I took on the landscaping business. I was 20 years old.

A couple of years went by and my life changed again. I got married and moved to a new town, so continuing with the landscaping business with my brother wasn't practical. I needed to look for another way to earn a living. I decided to become a driving instructor.

This set me on the teaching route and I quickly had to learn my own way of doing that. I was taught to teach in a very Dot to dot method. Again this went back to the school learning style of getting the essentials right in a strict order to pass the test. However this does not create good drivers. Pupils were concentrating more on their hand position on the wheel than planning ahead and deciding the best course of action. I didn't like this, so I developed my own style which enabled me to teach the real life driving of cause and effect. Your technique doesn't matter as long as you are safe and under control.

I've been a driving instructor since 2005 and decided during the first COVID lockdown of 2020 to use that instructional knowledge to teach and guide woodworkers on YouTube. I created a channel called 'King bespoke creations'. Here I have the freedom to pass on my experience to those who seek it out, and you don't have to write an essay or pass an exam at the end of the video! I have projects, weekend jobs and quick technique guides on my channel, and as you will find out if you subscribe, you will also see me taking a project into another direction should a mistake or inconvenient knot pop up.

When you start making for yourself, You either love what you have made, or you learn from the mistakes and try again! Every project you start is like a competition with yourself, and the prize is the item you make. The best thing about this competition is the more times you enter, the better the prize becomes!

Chapter 1
What is 'Self-taught'?

o what exactly does the phrase self-taught actually mean? Here's a dictionary definition of the phrase:

"Having acquired knowledge or skill on one's own initiative rather than through formal instruction or training."

Concise English Dictionary

It's very easy to hear the phrase 'Self-taught' and assume there was no external information used. Let's crush that myth straight away that it means locking yourself away from people and the internet. If we look at anyone who tells you they are self-taught or maybe self-made, do we believe they never once got outside assistance? If we look at the definition it says "on one's own initiative." This means you went looking for the answer. Yes you probably had a thought of your own first, but then hit a wall and couldn't find a solution.

So you ask.

Whether you ask a friend who has some interest in what you are trying to achieve, buy a book on the subject (just like this one!), search the internet or maybe even sign up to a night school course that you're sure will provide the information you need. Any of these methods came from your own initiative. There is an interest there and a wanting of understanding.

And I believe that is the key word here, understanding. There is a difference between learning and understanding. You can learn a solution or answer without truly understanding it. Often when we are taught by others we learn answers and information relating to that subject. When I was in school I could be presented with a Maths question, use the correct formula and give you the answer. But it meant nothing. I didn't know why the formula worked or what it could be useful for.

It was only when I decided to make my own snare drum (yes, I like to 'hit things with sticks') that I finally used Pi for a purpose. I needed to make a jig that would hold laminated Oak veneers in a perfect 14" circle. Maths finally gave me the answer as to how long each veneer needed to be. Who knew Pi had a use? Not me, not before this point! It was just a number. To get an answer. To pass a test.

Let's look at some of these different methods to build your understanding.

Doing it on you own

As I've said, this isn't the exclusive method of self-learning, however I do believe it's a very good one. It's simplest benefit is that anything you figure out for yourself will stay with you for a long time. Many different parts of the brain are engaged through this process.

Thinking about a problem for example will often get you a solution, or close to one. If you then sketch or write down what your thinking, another part of the brain is used and you see what the issues are in front of you. This will help you to see everything in perspective, see other problems and make it easier to correct them.

Moving things on further to a hands on trial and error scenario will greatly increase the understanding of what it is you are working on.

Once I had created my first Mortise and Tenon joint for example, I knew where the friction was. I could feel the strength in the joint. I could see where the two pieces would never move and which directional forces could pull them apart. But I could also see where there were issues. Places I could have cut more accurately to give a better hold or even just to improve the appearance.

Yes, this book is based on woodworking skills, but honestly this is true for almost any interest you would like to understand more. Especially anything practical.

Find out an answer

Often when we try to understand something new, our brain can't make the leap to the answer all on its own. So this is when we go and find an answer, or even part of an answer, to assist ourselves putting everything in place. How many times have you struggled to do something, then someone shows you a small piece of information and everything else just falls into place. Without that little piece of acquired knowledge you may have been running into a wall again and again. Those "Why didn't I think of that" moments allow us to see everything else clearly and we can fit it all in a line and move forward.

In the age we live in, answers are everywhere. Google, YouTube, Instagram, Pinterest, the list is huge and forever growing. You will soon know the sources that provides you with the quality answers you are looking for.

Often when you're looking for answers, on YouTube for example, you will find a whole new technique you find interesting. Go and try it! Understand it. But don't let it be set in stone, adapt it to fit you. I have watched Masters at work, showing me how they do it, but sometimes I find it doesn't sit well with me when I try it. I could use the specific technique but it didn't feel comfortable. It would make more sense for me to change the order of the tasks, or maybe leave a section out I thought was unnecessary. Sometimes changing things works, sometimes it doesn't, but now I understand why it needs to be done that way. Don't just blindly copy, because then you have one fixed skill instead of the starting point to ten others.

I'm sure you've done this too. Watched how to do something from five different experts and poured hours of watch time into the subject. The theory knowledge is there and you feel you understand it completely. However, until you go and try it, you will never truly understand it. If I watch the greatest guitar tutors explain soloing techniques. Learn all about music theory. Watch how to string any musical scale together to create the worlds greatest guitar solo, I will never be able to play it fluidly until I pick up a guitar and play it. Over and over and over again.

Take a class

I'll be honest, this isn't a solution I have used very often. There are some courses and teachers I would love to have studied with. People who's brain I would pick! Unfortunately time constraints often get in the way and the best courses can be expensive. And let's be honest, I'm a Yorkshireman so spending is always painful!

There are many small companies that have developed an education side to their business, and these usually are run in a very friendly hands-on manner. Often in a crafting niche, glass making or basket weaving for example they can be a day or weekend beginner course. If you enjoy it, you ask more questions and dive deeper. More complicated projects might start with a weeks course and head into months if you want to get as much out of the Pro teachers as you can.

Many colleges hold practical evening classes. If they are in the subjects you want to learn, look into them. Find out what level they do and who the instructor is. If I'm asking for help I want it to be from someone who has been in that field for a number of years. I don't want to learn from someone who has studied the theory and just passes that information along.

There are also lots of formal education establishments now offering courses on a self-learning basis too. Allowing you to go at your own pace and learn in your favoured style. This would be good to gain the big university degrees, if you don't feel the standard way of learning in lecture halls works for you.

My advice for, any course you might sign up for, is to keep in mind the reason you sought out the course in the first place. If it is for more than just the qualification then take the information you're given and make sure you understand it. Ask questions. Take notes. Do your own trial of the information provided.

Above all remember it was your need for answers and understanding that brought you along. Make sure you fulfil that before you are signed off.

Use one, some, or all

There is no right or wrong way of learning. We all learn in different ways and those ways might change from one project to another. I believe the more you can physically do for yourself, the greater the understanding will be. But even when the information has come from another source, by practically applying it, your understanding will deepen.

As your hands start to create and feel, your knowledge becomes more than theory. If I needed brain surgery for example (and some might argue I do!) I would rather have a surgeon that didn't do brilliantly on their exams but has a 98% success rate in theatre, than the world's greatest theoretical surgeon that has never held a knife!

To see and feel your thoughts makes it real. Get out there and try it. Repeat it again and look at what could be done better. Change the order of how you were taught to complete a task, if that order feels odd to you. Question everything! If the directions of others work well for you, go with them, that's why you asked for help. But don't just take it as right and everything else is wrong.

The next step is to look at how you could change aspects of it to suit a different need. This is where we truly start to build our self knowledge and allow ourselves to grow in our chosen field. Or in woodworking terms, build anything we can think of.

Chapter 2
Wood and Tools

---

k, so now we get to the part about woodwork. To be able to choose the correct technique for our project, we need to understand our materials.

Wood and tools. How do they interact with each other? Do we need to use every tool and every species of timber to know how to create something? You'll be glad to hear the answer is No!

There are thousands of tools out there and new inventions coming out constantly, telling us we need this product to improve our craft. There are even more types of wood species that we can use to build with. So how can we know what is best when we set out to make something? Let's strip it down to the basics, the bare essentials that can be added to later.

Understanding wood

I'm sure you've heard that wood species can be placed into two types, Softwood and Hardwood. This is technically true, but what does that really mean and how does it help us.

Firstly the names themselves are a little misleading. Hardwood does not always mean the wood is harder than Softwood. Look at Balsa wood for example. Often used in model aircraft making for its incredible strength to weight ratio, most people wouldn't call it a hard wood, but it is in fact a Hardwood.

The distinction is more about the tree than the wood itself. Hardwoods generally come from deciduous trees that lose their leaves each year, and softwood usually comes from evergreens.

For us as woodworkers we can often tell by the price! Softwoods (Pine for example) are easy to get hold of and are cheaper to buy because they grow faster and are quicker to process and dry. Hardwoods on the other hand are usually much more expensive. Taking longer to grow and be processed, they also have a greater tendency to be stable when working with them and look beautiful.

Those beautiful looks usually come from grain patterns. Take a Hardwood like Maple. It can look very boring and plain, but when the lumber yard knows what to look for and how to cut the tree to maximum effect, you can see wonders in the grain that can appear three dimensional. Terms like 'flame' or 'quilted' can look like a beach that's been rippled by the sea and will be guaranteed to make your build look amazing.

Softwoods can have some figuring in the grain but are often by chance and are usually very faint. They are generally very straight grained and other than finding a knot, will be very predictable to work with.

If you pick a length of pine you will see the grain running along it's length. You can split the wood along those grain lines very easily, you can predict where the split will continue. This happens because of the fast growing nature of softwoods. Run your fingernail across the grain, you will find it sinks into the lighter coloured parts and doesn't in the darker lines. This where the tree grew quickly in the summer (lighter colour) and slower in the winter (darker harder lines).

In Hardwoods you may get a different response when splitting the grain and some, like Oak can be quite predictable. However many have a complex grain structure that cris-crosses and splits quite randomly. Iroko for instance has a grain pattern running in opposing directions across its width. This means you will be working with the grain AND against the grain in a span of less than 5cm. But again, after using it, you will be able to see which way it works and apply that knowledge to other woods when you see the same patterns in the grain.

There is a common thought that Softwoods are easier to work with than Hardwoods. In some aspects that is true. Sawing through Softwood is definitely easier than Hardwood. However, a Hardwood will produce a cleaner cut and more prices joint with ease and practice.

If we look at Pine versus Oak, we can easily see how a chisel will cut through pine quicker as it slices through the fibres. However as pine is softer it also chips and gets dented scruffy edges, compressing the fibres and giving a joint that can easily have a visible gap. Oak does not do this. When performing exactly the same tasks on oak you find the edges stay crisp, every cut is more precise and the finished piece will be of better quality. To improve the work on pine, your tools actually have to be sharper to make sure they slice through wood without crushing any fibres.

Wood choice in a project will often come down to looks, and it's always exciting to work with a new species for the first time. My advise when you do this is to buy a little extra piece to test some of these qualities. Does it split in a predictable manner? Does it plane easily? Does your normal finish work well? All of this testing adds up to a greater understanding of your materials. Giving you a superior finished product and an increased knowledge ready to use on your next project.

Tools for understanding

When I first got into woodworking I did the same thing a lot of people do, I bought lots of power tools! Drills, saws, sanders and even some workshop machinery. I thought that's what I needed, because that's what they use in factories, on building sites and even on many TV shows and YouTube (not that YouTube was a thing back then!). These tools make repeated jobs easier and speed up the process without requiring great skill. They also make an unholy amount of noise and dust, and if used with too much trust can put you in the emergency room very quickly!

Safety glasses, hearing protection and dust masks are essential with these tools in a small workshop or shed. I learned after a few years that constantly having to put on PPE was a chore! I realised that I started reaching for a hand saw instead of using the table saw, just to avoid putting on safety wear. I used a hand plane instead of the belt sander to avoid choking on dust clouds. It was then I realised I really enjoyed using them! I found a new love of working cleanly at a volume I could listen to the radio, and found it often created a better finished project because of it too.

But the biggest change was my understanding of what was actually happening with every cut. A power tool just rips through the wood, almost without concern as to the structure of the timber. With a hand tool we know which way the grain is running, where the strength will be, or not be, inside the joints. We then start to look for these grain lines before we start to cut. We take the time to find out the greatest directional strength and also start to pick out the most attractive sides you want to see when the build is done. In short, our skills and understanding of how tools and wood work best together, goes through the roof!

What tools do we really need?

Which tools we would like, and what tools we actually need are two different things! We would love a huge workshop with every tool ever made that might be perfect for that one specific task. In reality we don't need very much at all. Let's have a look at what you actually need to get started.

Saw   A saw is vital, and an inexpensive one from your local hardware store will do just fine. We can look at getting specific cross cut saws (cutting across the grain) and rip cut saws (cutting along the grain) later when we want to invest and build our arsenal. A modern saw will have hardened steel teeth which stay sharp for a long time. The downside to this is that when they do get blunt it's impossible to sharpen them, resulting in a shopping trip to the store again. I tend to buy two or three saws a year using this method. Vintage saws don't have hardened teeth, so they need to be sharpened with a small file. Not a hard job but one that might need to be done every week if your using it a lot.

Chisel A chisel is another must have tool. They can vary in price massively. From £10 for a pack of 6 to over £80 each. I found spending £15 - £20 each generally gets you something with a quality steel and pleasant wooden handle. I personally have been using Rider chisels (not sponsored!) for the last few years and have been very impressed with them. A 12mm/ 1/2" chisel will be a great starting size, but you will soon want all the sizes!

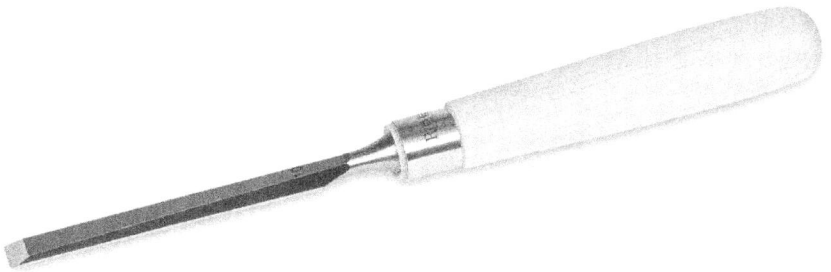

Plane A hand plane is a treat to use. After years of pummelling through wood with a belt sander to get the correct thickness and a smooth finish, switching to a plane is instantly more satisfying. Often quicker, always quieter and usually giving a better finish. A freshly sharpened blade on a well set plane will eliminate the need for any fine sanding. A glass like finish achieved with minimal fuss. I would always recommend finding an old Stanley or Record No.4 as they are plentiful and cheaper than a new one. They are also vastly superior too! Made from a much better quality steel and using better manufacturing methods, a vintage plane will last forever. If you want to buy new, you need to spend a lot of money from companies such as Veritas.

Both chisels and plane blades are only ever as good as the last time it was sharpened. Learning how to sharpen quickly and effectively keeps you safer, as you'll need less force to use them, and give cleaner cuts.

Drill   When it comes to putting a round hole through a piece of wood, you pretty much need a drill! I have a few old hand drills that I enjoy using, but this where modern battery powered drills with quick change chucks, probably win out over the vintage models.

These four items will get you building almost anything. There might be another tool that is more specific to the task, but one of these tools could probably do it too. There is one more group of tools that you will use on every job you work on, and they are measuring and marking tools.

Measure, measure, cut

Measuring your work and marking out where to cut really is essential for any project in the shed. A tape measure is obviously a great place to start, but you use rulers of all sizes more often than you might think. Not all rulers are equal though! Try to find metal ones with laser cut markings rather than printed numbers and lines. I would definitely have a 12"/30cm ruler and a 1m ruler ready to go. I also have 24"/60cm and 6"/15cm rulers, not essential but it's amazing how often I reach for them instead of the two standard sizes.

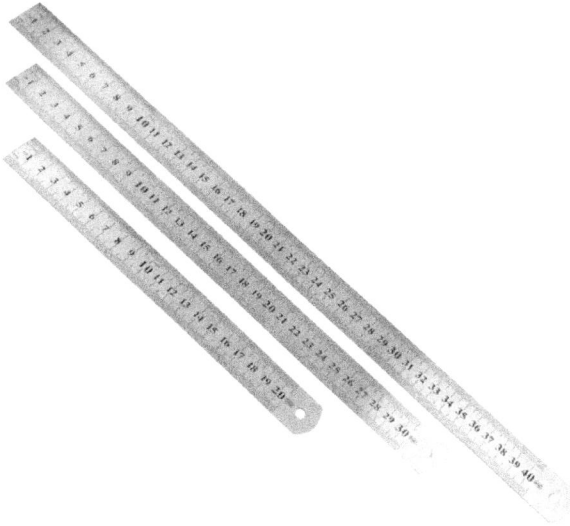

A measuring tool I use everyday is a Combination square. These have a 90* and 45* edge to them that can slide across a ruler, giving accurate and repeatable layouts every time.

Often when we start in woodwork we often reach for a pencil to mark out the cuts before heading for our tools. Whilst it's important to mark off, a better tool for the job is a marking knife. A knife will give more accurate lines (even a pencil line can be too thick) and will actually give the saw or chisel somewhere to track as you start. I admit I was reluctant to use a knife at first, wondering if I'm marking the wood in the wrong place, but once you start to use one you won't go back to a pencil for anything other than rough cutting chipboard!

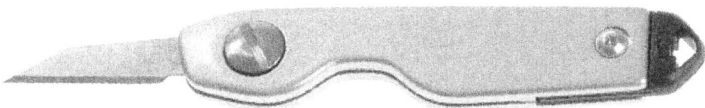

Chapter 3
The three essential joints

———————————————————————————————

I believe there are three woodworking joints that become the backbone of all projects. These essential joints that, when understood, can be manipulated to suit your needs and help you to create any project.

Now with any woodworking project, there's a few tricks that should become a set part of your process. The first is this, always mark off your cuts with the actual wood you're joining instead of just a tape measure width. Learn this trick early and your carpentry will instantly be more accurate. A 2x4 is never 2x4! Timber widths are always nominal and by the time you've smoothed it down, will be fractionally less still. By using the actual piece you're going to join, you guarantee it's the correct width.

So, let me introduce the essential joints to you. Say hello to the Half-lap, the Mortice and Tenon, and the Dovetail joints. These joints are strong and beautiful. Get used to them and they will be your companions in the workshop for ever!

Make sure to watch the videos of these joints to see them in action and get a few ideas as to where they could lead.

Half-lap joint

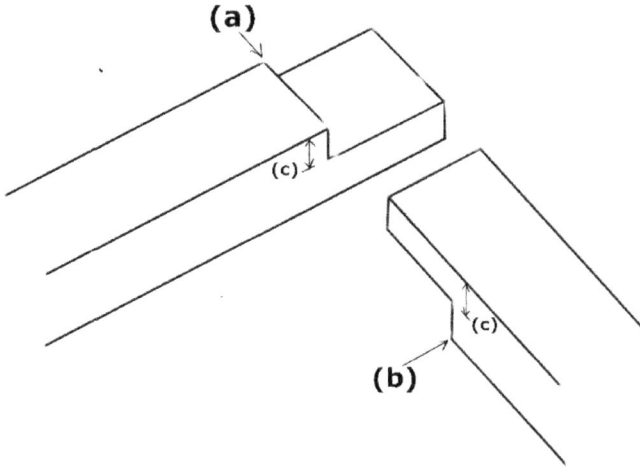

(a)

(b)

(c)

(c)

The Half-lap joint is probably the simplest way of joining two pieces of timber. It is often used as a corner joint, but can be used anywhere along the length. This joint provides good structural strength and a large surface area for wood glue.

Essentially all you're doing is cutting both pieces of timber in half and placing them together. This overlap allows the frame (or whatever you're making) to stay the same thickness instead of having one timber sat on top of another.

To mark out this joint, hold the pieces across from each other and lightly mark the edges of the top plank, then using a square, mark the full straight line with the knife (a). Flip the pieces and do the same to the other plank (b).

To cut to the correct depth it's best to use a Mortise Gauge, but if you don't have one just make sure the depths are measured from the top of each piece for a perfect fit (c). This measurement then doesn't actually need to be perfectly central, just even on both parts.

Once the the marking is done it's time to cut. Use a saw to cut from lines (a) and (b) down to the 'halfway' line (c). At this point you have an option, you can either use the saw and cut along line (c) or get a chisel and chip the waste out. I love using the chisel for this, as it's often quicker and easier, and again you will understand the way the wood is oriented. Getting to know the grain directions.

Start halfway through the waste section and chip from both edges towards the centre. Keep splitting the waste in half until you are shaving down to the line. Once you have done this on both pieces, have a test fit to see if the timbers go together well and you have a pretty good feeling of level. If the two pieces have a lip on them, you may need to take a little more off.

When you're happy with your joint, squeeze a little wood glue on one side of all connecting surfaces and hold the joint together. Using clamps or a vice, making sure the joint doesn't slip, let the glue set before final run over with a plain or sander to level up.

Your joint is complete! After repeating this joint a few times you will start to get yourself a system of marking and cutting that works for you. You will then be able to see how to adapt this joint to fit your needs. Maybe your wood looks too thick, or it needs to be placed at a different angle?

You have a 'tool' to use for any number of projects, change and adapt it however you feel is necessary!

Mortice and Tenon Joint

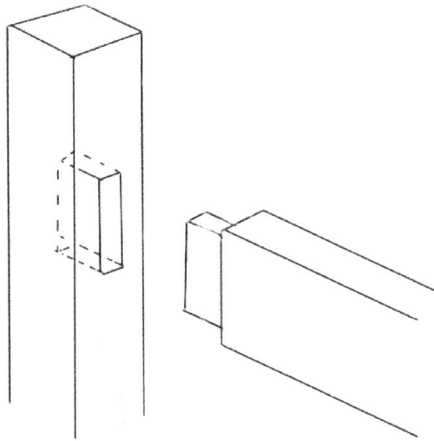

The Mortise and Tenon joint is, in its simplest form, used to connect a beam to a post. The tongue (Tenon) fits into the mouth (Mortice) and creates a very strong joint that can be adapted in a great number of ways. The tenon might fit part of the way through the post, or all the way through. It might be glued in place for a permanent hold or pegged to allow removal or seasonal wood movements. That peg could be placed through the side of the post, or through the tenon as it pokes out of the other side. So many options and uses, it really is an essential joint.

To mark out, first we need to work on the tenon. It needs to be between half and two thirds the thickness of the beam with an even size shoulder on all four sides. Importantly for ease of work, the tenon needs to be the same thickness as one of your chisels. This makes cutting the Mortise hole a lot simpler.

Mark the lines square on each side (d) and the depth lines on each face (e). Using a saw, cut the shoulder lines on each side then remove the excess to get down to depth on all four sides. Exactly the same way the half-lap was done.

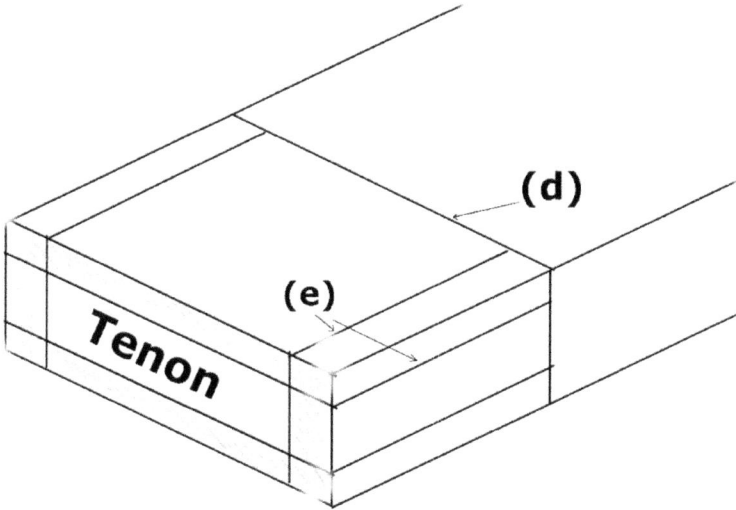

Once the tenon is cut, we use it to mark the position and exact size of the Mortise hole to be cut. Again use a marking knife to cut the edges of the hole.

This is where we use a different technique! Holding the chisel 90 degrees to the wood and with the bevel side of the chisel on the waste side of the cut (f), lightly tap it to make the first slice. Keep moving the chisel along the length of the Mortise, no more than 1mm at a time. By moving such small increments you'll only need to tap the chisel lightly each time to cut deeper and deeper with each strike. Once down to the correct depth or you've reached the end of the marking, turn the chisel around and head back to the other end.

Once the Mortise is cut to depth all the way through, test fit the tenon. It should be quite snug, maybe needing a little persuasion with a mallet to get it in. If it feels too tight, check the sides of the Mortice are straight and clean then try again.

It might take a few goes to get it right, but once you've mastered this joint you will regularly choose it to construct many different projects, and with all the different variations you can think of to meet your needs.

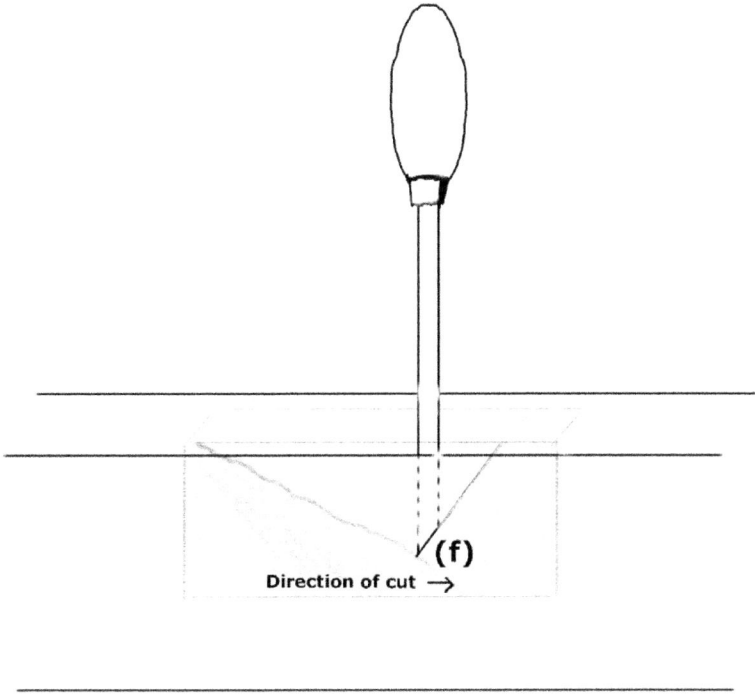

(f)

Direction of cut →

Dovetail joints

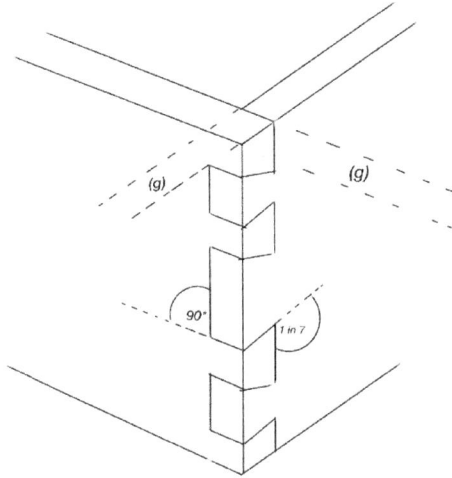

Dovetail joints are for showing off! Well not quite. Modern glues have made it much quicker and easier to cut a recess and glue two pieces of wood together, than to hand cut some attractive yet still very functional dovetails. Often seen in smaller items like trinket boxes and for attaching drawer fronts, this joint is perfect for connecting two flat pieces of timber at 90 degrees.

This is definitely the more difficult joint of the three, but once you've practiced them, you'll want to put them everywhere!

There are two main types. A 'Through Dovetail' where the joint is seen on both sides and is generally used for making boxes. And a 'Half-lap Dovetail' which is only seen on the sides, regularly used on drawer fronts. The half can be used for many other things, including as a replacement for a Mortise and tenon where you want the joint to be seen.

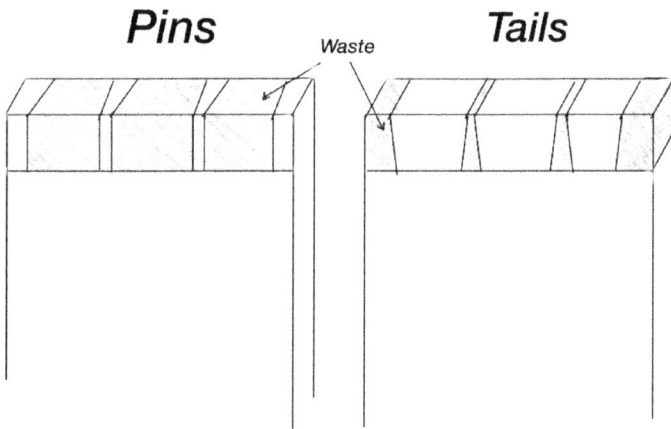

Pins   *Waste*   **Tails**

This is definitely a joint that's easier to 'watch' than 'read' how to mark off! But let's have a go.

A through dovetail is measured with the actual thickness of each board (g). Mark each board lightly all the way round, this will give the depth of the tails and pins.

Now, there is constant discussion as to whether the tails or pins should be marked first. I suspect it doesn't make a huge difference. I find if I get used to marking the tails first with a through joint, it makes it easier when we move onto a half lap joint later.

It's been found over the years that a dovetail's optimal angle is around 1 in 7. So let's start there and play with it later in future projects. There is no set number of dovetails that need to be marked out. More tails means more surface area, but too many will be fragile and could snap.

They also don't have to be the same size, in fact a modern trend is to make sure they are different to show they were hand cut and not done on a machine. Once the tails are marked out, cut out the waste with a saw and a chisel. Be careful and make sure all of the cut sides are square to the face. Anything less than square will leave you with gaps in the finished joint.

With the tails cut out, lay them on the edge of the other board. Use a marking knife to carefully scribe around the tails. Once marked, again use a saw and chisel to cut out the waste. When both the tails and pins have been cut, try them together. Again we're looking for a snug fit, possibly needing a light tap. If the joint can be put together with very little effort, then the gaps are too big. If it's too tight or simply won't go fit, then a little slicing with a chisel is needed to join them together.

Once you're happy with the fit, it only takes a little glue on the connecting sides to fix the joint forever. An incredibly strong and beautiful joint is now in your repertoire to be used and changed as you see fit. Some carpenters almost have a signature style of dovetail, some have curved edged tails or even have them as letters.

Chapter 4
The challenge

Set yourself a challenge that you don't know how to complete! I did when I first decided I liked woodworking, my learning curve was steep and I developed a style that is still part of my work now. Let me tell you a story.

When I was 20 years old, after quitting university and moving back home, I decided I wanted a new bed. Having not done any joinery before I obviously decided I would build one! It had to be a double bed, but also longer than a standard bed. At 6'2" I was sick of my feet poking out of the end during the night and getting cold toes! So the first problem to solve was how to make the bed longer but still use a readily available mattress size that would be easy to source and not needing to be specially made? That would be enough of a challenge you would think, but no!

I decided to ban the use of **screws, nails or glue** throughout the entire build!

Why I decided to challenge myself with these restrictions, I'm not sure, but my thought process was that it must be possible. People joined wood together before these items were invented, I just needed to figure out how. I roughly knew what a Mortise and Tenon joint was, but had never tried one and didn't know how to make sure it stayed together without glue. But again I knew it had to be possible.

Material choice was simple, I would use the 2x4 and 4x4 pine planks from the builders merchant. It would be thick and heavy. Just the way I like furniture to be. I also wanted to put a little carving on the headboard, so it wasn't totally utilitarian.

So here's my challenge to you for the next 10-15 minutes:

<u>Design my bed.</u>

This is the criteria:

1) material is limited to readily available pine
2) Double bed width
3) Extra 10" in length whilst using a standard mattress
4) Must have an integrated headboard

5) No screws, nails or glue

Grab a piece of paper and try to think of how this might go together. Which joints could you use? How will you have a longer bed without using a custom mattress? Once you have an idea, turn over and see if it matches my build.

How did you get on? I'd love to know if your design is anything like my design. And I love the fact that there will be hundreds of new bed designs being drawn up around the world right now!

So let's go through my solutions.

1) **Materials**. First it was the simple matter of ordering the wood, as I was regularly in the builders merchant for the landscaping work it was easy to grab the stuff I would require. I treated myself to a new saw too!

2) **Width**. A simple look at mattress sizes gave me the dimensions I needed for the width of the bed

3) **Length**. Ok, so here's where we start getting specific. I figured the extra 10" of length I wanted could be placed at the head end of the bed. Having the pillows on the mattress, seemed like a waste of prime real estate! So I would build an extension block the same height as a mattress for my pillows to sit on. This would give me the full mattress for my body to lie on and keep my feet from dangling over the edge!

4) **Headboard**. For the headboard I would have taller legs than the foot end. Four 2x4 beams would be joined to the legs so that they stand on top of each other, maybe I could use thin plywood inserted between them to stop any movement (later I found this was called a biscuit joint).

5) **Restrictions**. The joints for the main frame would be the trusty Mortise and Tenon. At the time I didn't know which part was the Mortice and which part was the Tenon, but that didn't matter. But how would it stay together? With a peg. This peg could could be large

doweling, available from the builders merchant, as its a large joint I'm cutting. I thought at first of creating the Mortise and Tenon then just drilling through it and hammering in the dowel. The problem I faced was that my joint would move when trying to drill, this would mean my joint would be pegged in the wrong place. I figured if I made the hole in the Tenon a little further back, it would actually pull the two pieces tighter together as the dowel was hammered through. Problem solved!

Actually one of the trickiest parts of this no screws part of the build was the slats that the mattress would sit on. How to stop them moving and sliding? Again I came back to using a dowel. I planned at first to insert the dowel at an angle to make it more difficult to move, this turned out to be unnecessarily complex and simply having the dowel in a tight fit was enough.

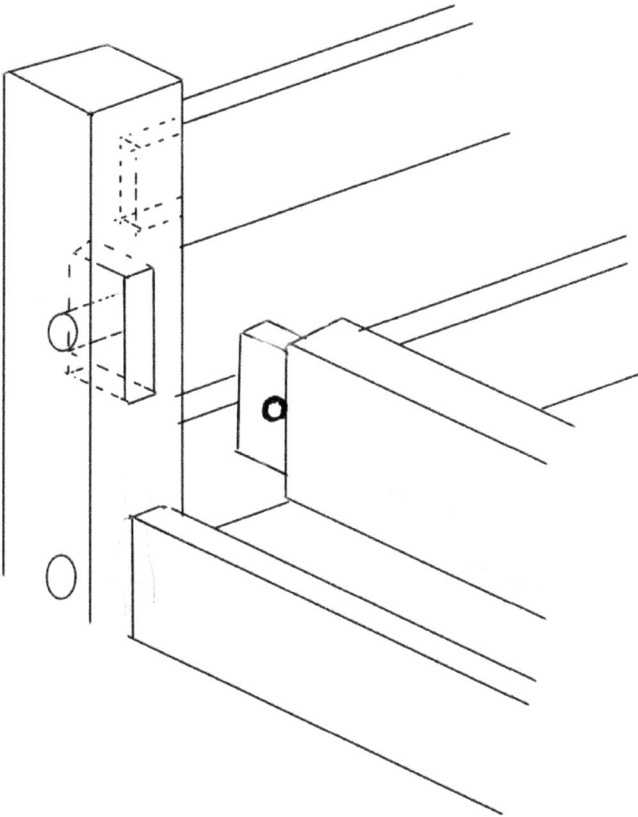

Challenge complete?

So did I complete the challenge? Yes! And more than just having a finished bed to sleep on, my understanding of the wood, joints and techniques skyrocketed. In this one project alone I had to make 22 pegged Mortise and Tenon joints. That's a lot of repetition. As I worked through each one, my accuracy increased and my method of cutting these joints became more efficient with each one completed. I went from never having cut a joint before to having a fairly good finished piece in a relatively small time. If I had been shown the exact way of cutting these joints from the beginning, I'm convinced I would not have understood what was happening inside the joint anywhere near as much as I did through my own practice and refinement.

Could I have made the bed better? Absolutely, in fact I have done it twice since that first bed. And created other beds in a different design, because I know what is and isn't achievable with the joints I've worked with.

Chapter 5

What now?

So what now? You've just read a book about being self taught. Did it tell you every minute detail you need, to complete a specific task? I hope not! That might sound like an odd thing for me to say, but I honestly believe you can head into your shed and start creating things with the knowledge you have '*Acquired through ones own initiative*' by purchasing this book. However, the knowledge you gained from reading a book isn't enough. You need to get practical. It's time to turn that knowledge into understanding by actually doing these joints, and others you can think of, again and again. Getting a little better each time. Don't be disappointed if the first time through, your work isn't perfect. See what you have achieved from nothing and be proud! Look at what you did and see where you could do it better next time. Adapting how and where these joints can be used to create anything you can think of.

And of course when you set out to intentionally teach yourself woodworking, you realise that you can be self taught in a vast variety of other subjects. Maybe you could take up another hobby? Maybe you could complete that project that you started but didn't have the knowledge or skill to finish?

Once your aware that you're capable of your own development, that it's not too late to learn something, life might just open more doors than you thought possible. When you realise that just because you didn't learn like everyone else at school or feel you missed out on certain subjects, your 'education' doesn't have to stop there. Set out to find some answers, make a start and see where it takes you.

So what challenge will you set yourself? What could you make that you don't currently know how to complete?

In my next book I'll be looking at how to embellish your woodworking with decoration. Skills like Carving, Pyrography and Inlays will be looked at. Hopefully you'll find another new way to love working with wood.

I hope self learning works for you, not just in woodworking but many aspects of life. So many things to learn, and with the world at your fingertips your new hobby could even provide you with a new career!

If you have an interest in something don't ever think it's too late to learn, or you cannot start because you don't have prior knowledge. Someone who is an expert in any subject was a beginner first! Now is the time to start. To take those first steps to gain your understanding.

About the Author

Living in the North of England, Chris Hattan has been working with wood since his late teens and has been a driving instructor for over 15 years. Since 2020 he has combined both of these attributes to create a YouTube channel that teaches people all about working with wood. Often using hand tools, showing that you don't need all the machinery, Chris has gained an appreciative audience that often comments how simple he makes it.

Printed in Great Britain
by Amazon

77394895R30032